An Ode…

Copyright© 2018 F. Renee Hamilton

All Rights Reserved

ISBN: 978-1-7327525-2-8

An Ode...

All Ways, Him 1

First 3

Wilderness 5

Things 9

Come 11

Expectancy 13

Still 17

Fit 19

Illusion 21

Untitled 25

Absence 27

Unnoticed 29

You 33

Untitled 35

Arrival 37

Captivity 39

Fault 43

Real 45

Miss, Understanding 47

Wait 49

Reality 51

Again 53

Lesser 57

F. Renee Hamilton

<u>All Ways, Him</u>

An Ode...

I said his name again...
To myself, clearly.
And it still felt like home.
I hadn't said it in a long time.
Yet there it was.
A soft utterance in the back of my mind.
His name hidden deep beneath the surface.
Comfortably residing in the land of once was,
Always standing guard at the gate of what could be.
It had been a while.
But there it was again.
A subtle warning it seemed.
As if foreshadowing some imminence.
First a whisper, then more frantic.
It took me away from my love.
I shook loose from his grip and let my mind wander.
I couldn't take the risk of saying it out loud.
I rolled over and said it into the pillow.
I had forgotten how sweet that name tasted.
It rolled off the tip of my tongue.
It jarred me from my senses.
Made me lose reason.
That name made me wild.
It was the name of my first true love.
I just don't know why I spoke it as I lay here with you.

F. Renee Hamilton

First

An Ode...

I fell in love with your energy.

Then,

I got lost in your auric layers,

before I even knew your last name.

Life's funny that way.

They say I'm impulsive when it comes to matters of the heart.

But maybe my soul recognized you,

from another place,

another time,

another life...

And I had no choice but to be drawn in.

Again.

This is an ode,

to all the men I have loved.

Or never planned to love thus far.

F. Renee Hamilton

<u>Wilderness</u>

I was in the wilderness.
Untamed, corybantic.
Grasping for an inkling of stability.
I wanted love.
I needed it more than the air I breathed.
I craved it.
It was the motivation behind my actions.
It was the catalyst to all my catastrophes.
I yearned for it.

That desire led me across barren lands.
My body was starved for nourishment.
My flesh torn.
Fingers mangled with abrasions.
Yet, I kept digging, looking, searching… trying to find some form of life amongst the lifelessness.

I wanted something with soul and substance.
I needed to feel.
Hearts beating, sweat dripping from brow, gentle kisses upon my face.
Warmth.

I dug until my nails were covered in dirt.
So soiled and dirty I could barely recognize myself.
I was still me, but a more tarnished version.
Harder.
Less refined.

Then finally I forced myself to move.

I walked into the darkness.
I knew what I needed, but still couldn't see.
I was veiled and bound.
My hands behind my back prevented me from touching, digging, exploring, looking to find more.

Still bound.
I just walked.
And I waited.

An Ode...

F. Renee Hamilton

Things

An Ode...

I'm intrigued by all the broken things.
Infatuated by the missing pieces that keep them from being whole.
Constantly consumed by their stories.
Fighting to stay afloat amidst my own.
I give a lot to fill them up.
Myself, constantly sacrificed to do my life's work.
I'm a healer, but when will they put back what was taken?
When will I find the healer whose purpose is to make me whole?

F. Renee Hamilton

<u>Come</u>

Your hand firmly around my neck keeps me in place.
The intensity of your body overwhelms me.
But this isn't the time for flight or fight, so I embrace your every move.
I don't run from it.
Penetration surpasses my body and fragments my soul.
I want you to consume me,
hungrily tear shreds of my body to sustain you from the longing you feel.
Share spaces and stories in perpetuity as you continue to climb deeper and deeper into my innermost.
We exchange glances and your eyes devour me.
You slow down, more confident behind each stroke.
You want me to feel your love
But at this moment all I feel is your piece.
Peace, in a moment of vicious tranquility.
I choke back I love you.
This is not the time or place to show emotion, as we are currently at war.
Fighting on the same side, awaiting the few seconds until the battle is finally won.
Waiting for the moment to come.

Expectancy

It was never your fault that my expectations transcended reality.
I let the fantasies and make-believe in my head automatically set a standard.
One that you would never be able to reach.
I set the bar too high.
Placed too many hoops for you to jump through.
Then got mad when you couldn't finish the course.
Strayed.
So many times, you wandered off the beaten path.
Took lefts that led to other women, rights that always brought you back to me.
Instead of waving my white flag in defeat I stayed.
Repetition.
It was too hard to let go.
I didn't want to give up or give in.
I just wanted you to be perfect, for us to be perfect to the world.
The world.
The world led me to believe that life was all about perfection.
I neglected the signs, I neglected myself, but most importantly I neglected you.
Life has taught me that maybe the end of us wasn't all on you.
Me and my desire for perfection share some of the blame too…
Running the same race for so many years can be hard on the body and even worse on the soul.
We were both tired.
Yet I wanted the world.
I cared more about how the world saw us than how we saw ourselves.
We were fighters.
We fought each other almost as hard as we loved each other.

But what we fought most was the fact that maybe we were just never meant to be together.
Or maybe we were, but let pride and pain cloud our judgment.
It was always easier to stay, the convenience, the comfort.
But every day made it harder on us.
I was too scared to give up.
You were mine and were always supposed to be.
I played victim a lot.
More than I should have, because you were just as hurt as me.
But it was just easier that way.
Stay, just stay.

An Ode...

F. Renee Hamilton

Still

An Ode...

It was at that moment that I felt least like myself.
It was as if I had been frozen in time.
Seeing, touching, hearing but not visualizing myself moving forward.
That stillness lingered.
It seeped through my pores and tickled my nose.
It irritated my senses.
It was the itch that I couldn't scratch.
It interrupted my sleep at night.
It was the blow that took the wind out of me.
It left me breathless.
It made me weary.
I was just still.

Fit

The jagged edges of your brokenness tear at the fabric of my soul.
The tighter I cling to you the more I rip at the seams.
I thought our broken pieces would fit together perfectly.
Two damaged, imperfect persons,
forcing puzzle pieces in place, our compatibility working as glue.
Our passionate kisses served the purpose of adhesive,
until I had convinced myself we were whole.
We molded as one when bodies combined, and you were the perfect fit.
You fit like a glove.
We fit.
Until we didn't.
I felt the exact moment when the threads came loose.
Piece by piece, the layers came apart.
The silk that once delicately tickled my spine, now felt rough as wool.
The colors that shined so brightly as your shirt hit the floor now hurt my eyes.
My limbs lost their way.
I could no longer find the parts of you that felt like home beneath my fingertips.
I felt exposed.
No longer shielded by your being.
Fully naked.
Bare.
No longer were we a fit.
No longer could I force it.

F. Renee Hamilton

<u>Illusion</u>

I still yearn for your illusion.
The ideas that you painted in my subconscious, they led me to believe there would be a happily ever after.
Now my time is just fragmented between before you and after you.
You were a magician.
Or was I the one who pulled rabbits from hats?
Waved around my wand to create the perfect fantasy in you.
Our world was perfect.
In the short time that we co-existed, I experienced bliss that no other man has been yet to hold a flame to.
You shined light on me.
I opened my eyes and saw love.
I felt love.
Your touch awakened parts of me that had been asleep for eternity.
You broke walls that had been built inside of me for a lifetime.
Making love in sacred spaces, us, unequivocally in tune with each other.
Sleeping in your arms was the purest form of euphoria.
Your touch.
Your smell.
Your energy.
Your fingertips.
Gently tracing our future down the small of my back.
Our forever.
I imagined it all.
It was my reality.
Then one day the smoke cleared.

F. Renee Hamilton

I looked out into the audience and you were nowhere to be found.
I was alone.
A one-woman act who had rehearsed every scene, every line.
A modern day make believe.
Yet a part of it was real.
Then the curtains closed.
And then all I was left with was a vision of you.

An Ode...

F. Renee Hamilton

Untitled

An Ode...

The last time we spoke,

I had tears in my eyes.

It felt good to release them.

Those tears freed me.

You questioned my emotion.

Told me to wash my face.

Used this opportunity.

Finally faded out of my life.

There was no consoling.

No words of affirmation.

Nothing to salvage the situation.

You seemed offended.

We parted ways.

I would never talk to you again.

Absence

An Ode...

I've grown accustomed to your absence.
But when you come, you fill voids within me that surpass the realm of doubt and reason.
I don't understand the attraction.
But when I think of you, I can't stop myself from wanting more, wanting it all.
This isn't enough.
But then it's everything, and the thought of losing it drives me insane.
I'm unfulfilled
But even though, I want and deserve more, I find myself content with the fragments of yourself you give me.
I'm not foolish.
But then, I find myself foolishly hanging on to your every word when I know I am worth action.
I can't start over again.
But then, I know I owe it to myself and deserve a forever.
You said you would give me the world.
But then, I know that together is just something we aren't meant to be.

Unnoticed

I would've walked right past you on a regular day,
my nose in the air,
eyes focused on the superficial.
I had a knack for those sorts of things.
The look good to you, but always bad for you.
I could spot them a mile away.
I tossed hair over shoulders,
pushing past all other possibilities.
Possibility.
Like many before me,
I'd been preconditioned to seek instead of waiting to be
sought.
Preconceived notions of yesteryear out the window,
I went for what I wanted.
Too impatient to wait for the he who finds her,
I clung to the he who wants her…
But just for a while,
or just for that night.
I did not know what I needed.
I did not know what I deserved.
I had lost sight of forever.
The present provided promise,
even though it was a temporary fix to an everyday desire.
Every day I desired the consistency,
the knowledge that feelings had not changed overnight.
The promise that you would still feel the same,
day after day, every morning,

always more, never less.
That ideal was an illusion,
or rather it was a phenomenon that never once made my acquaintance.
I had given up.
Pledged to live a life of mediocrity,
made peace with all the pieces people were willing to share of themselves with me.
Temporarily.
I couldn't recognize forever in the state I was in.
It took time. It took focus. It took heartache.
It took you.

An Ode...

F. Renee Hamilton

<u>You</u>

I think it was the softness of your stare that made me take notice.
You looked past my exterior and locked eyes with who I truly was.
Then your touch.
Your firm grip gave me security.
Your fingertips brought simplistic pleasure to the most obscure places.
The caress of my ankle.
The interlocking of fingers.
Us sitting still,
being,
existing on the same plane.
Unequivocal acknowledgment of each other's presence,
subconsciously playing a role in each other's story.
Our story.

F. Renee Hamilton

<u>Untitled</u>

I lived on hope.

I hoped for the best from everyone.

For a man to respect the process.

To respect me.

To respect the covenant.

You shed light on potential.

On possibly being reality.

For once there was a true chance of realness.

And then I pinched myself.

I didn't want to be lost in the moment.

I wanted to enjoy it.

Say farewell to fairytales.

You and I, we are real.

We had to be.

You told me so.

Arrival

An Ode...

I can't say that I prayed for your arrival.
You were unexpected,
an atypical reflection of everything I needed,
but never thought I'd have.
As a matter of fact,
I didn't know I needed you.
I didn't choose you.
I had never sought after one with your expertise.
I never fathomed the idea that someone existed who was so well versed in the art of loving me.
I almost missed the opportunity, I almost let the unknown persuade me back into the realm of already experienced.
The already failed at.
But opportunity – and fate – were on my side.
The unexpected changed my life, it changed my course, it changed my heart.
It changed me.
To think that every closed door and detour led me to you makes me glad for the journey.
My final destination.
At a steady pace.

Captivity

He was in captivity.

Confinement.

Married to a life lacking fulfillment.

Ebbs and flows of good times kept him pacified.

Kept him from breaking free of his restraints.

Made him still.

Trapped.

Four walls surrounded him.

Surrounded her.

But she was free.

Going about life.

Taking for granted that caged being that needed air, needed light, needed love, needed life.

He saw no hope.

Only bondage.

Indentured.

Playing roles that made sense from the outside looking in, but fragmented his soul to the core

Freedom.

It looked like love.

It felt like appreciation.

But it escaped him.

Escape.

The possibility outweighed the maybes.

Chance and opportunity.

Maybe he deserved better.

The idea sounded foreign to him.

It chipped away at his confidence.

Bored holes into his esteem.

Made him question his masculinity.

F. Renee Hamilton

Almost broke him.
Completely.

F. Renee Hamilton

<u>Fault</u>

I would be lying if I said I was not thankful for her downfalls.
I find myself giddy filling up that emptiness she created in you.
Her missteps, miscalculations.
Misconceptions.
All of that paved the way for my soul to intervene.
To set you free, to give you peace.
For you to be seen.
And, loved by me.
Every insecurity she created in you was meticulously designed.
Particularly and exceptionally crafted for my undoing.
You see, all the shit she took for granted, I'd been yearning for.
Continuously.
Painstakingly perfecting my craft, my role, my reason, to accept it all.
I was meant to fix all the damage she had done.
We were both preparing.
In different spaces.
Different places.
Just waiting for the me and the you.
That girl did us both a favor.
Losing the best thing that's ever happened to me.
Caused hurt and pain that every day I get the privilege of making go away.
We make each other better.
Fix one another.
I just should have asked if you were at fault, too.

F. Renee Hamilton

<u>Real</u>

An Ode...

I needed to know we were real.
Not some illusion created in my head.
Nothing mirroring the white picket fences and happily ever after of fairytales.
Real, with substance.
Fragmented pieces haphazardly placed together molded by our experiences.
Real life, real feelings.
Behind the mask of rose-colored glasses all the smoke and mirrors gone, exposed.
Us, two different people, not perfect but determined to work.
After conflict, through it.
Contrite and compromised reality.
Realness, resolutions.
So that now, our love story can truly begin.

F. Renee Hamilton

Miss, Understanding

An Ode...

I heard what you were saying.

Dissected every word.

Understood each utterance.

Took note of every adjective.

Ingested each verb.

Made sense of pronouns, adverbs.

Truly understood.

Comprehended exactly what you had stated.

Then twisted your words into what I wanted to hear.

It didn't take much provocation.

Words catapulted me.

A different time, a different place.

I lost track of where I was.

Forgot who I was with.

Seconds of irrationality.

Minutes of hardheadedness.

Hours wasted not listening.

A few days of disbelief.

A week of doubt.

Almost an end to us.

It probably should have been.

Wait

Patiently she waits, pause then break.

Shifts constantly, heavy to the left.

Redistribute to the right.

Carrying, carrying.

Burdens so heavy, she just wants light.

Reality

I thought loving you was enough to sustain me.
I thought my all was enough to keep my bed warmed by you.
Knowing glances and the comfort of familiarity should've kept us in sync.
New adventures, inside jokes,
I thought were enough to keep your interest piqued.
Prime and ready.
Ready for us to just keep loving, just loving, each other.
Love is what I thought you needed.
I thought we both needed it.
I thought we were both content with simply that.
Just love was enough to carry us throughout a lifetime.
But you wanted to be.
In love.
Or not...
Because regardless of how unconditional.
The thought of being in just sounded better...
To you.
Better than.
Love.

F. Renee Hamilton

<u>Again</u>

I knew the moment I lost you.
It was a Wednesday night.
I was waiting for you.
Our routine carelessly flowed like a river, but that night there was a rip in the current.
I knew there was a problem after the first unanswered call.
I panicked.
I walked aimlessly around my living room until I fell to my feet.
It was as if all the wind had been knocked out of me.
I doubled over in excruciating pain.
When I was finally able to stand steadily on my own, it was too late.
I couldn't feel you.
That piece of you that had been tucked away safely in the depths of my being.
My cord, my intergalactic connection to you, our tie, was gone.
Severed.
That night was the first time that I couldn't sense your being.
Most mornings I could feel your arms around me.
Even when we were apart.
The heat that radiated from your body always warmed me like a cup of our favorite tea.
I could feel you waking up.
I could feel the start of your day.
I'd sniff your hair, deeply inhale your scent from the pillow and just know that all was well.
If you felt bad, that cord would gently tug as if to let me know that you needed me.
Most nights I could hear you say my name, always minutes before my phone would ring.

Your sleepy voice spoke to me.
It soothed me.
I could feel your weariness.
I always felt the strain of your day.
Regardless of time or space I could feel you, and that night you were gone.
I felt nothing.
I thought I'd be able to reason with you.
Unfortunately, you spoke a language that was no longer our own.
You shut me out.
I wanted to know if you were in distress, but dishevelment laced your voice.
It was the first time you wouldn't talk to me.
You said you couldn't.
You wouldn't explain.
You had a lot on your mind.
Too much to share at the moment.
It was the first night I cried myself to sleep over you.
The first of many.
The next day we made amends.
You told me you loved me.
Your hands felt the same.
Your lips found familiar places.
I still couldn't feel you.
You lifted me in the air and ferociously pounded your body into mine.
It wasn't our usual love making.
It was primitive.

Almost painful, but I felt you trying to make your presence known again to my body.
Inside of me, brutally so, and then you came.
Even though you had arrived, you still weren't there.
As such, I never felt you again.
That space for you, left barren.
Then it was Thursday…

F. Renee Hamilton

<u>Lesser</u>

A lesser woman would have no problem picking up where I left off.
Stepping in, in the midst of, with no respect for lines being crossed.
A lesser woman would not care that your hand was just holding mine.
That your fingers just touched my lips, as your tongue traced up my spine.
A lesser woman would have no qualms overlooking those things that were inherently me.
The scent of my perfume on your pillows, or on the blanket you covered me with when I fell asleep.
A lesser woman would be able to walk beside you with her head held up with pride.
Disregarding the promises you made me, every morning, and every night we laid side by side.
A lesser woman would have watched with envy romanticizing our every move.
Looking for moments to insert herself because instead of me, she thought she should be with you.
A lesser woman would have listened to every single word you said.
Reassuring your doubts, and playing up to the fantasies in your head.
A lesser woman would not care about the time I invested in you.
She would just see the fruits of my labor, but not truly know

what all I had to do.
A lesser woman would be happy with the prize she thought she had won.
Overlooking the fact that to win, serious damage had to be done.
A lesser woman would be okay with the fact that without me, there would not be this version of you.
I made you more desirable, and in my light shined this illusion of you.
A lesser woman would be willing to spend her life forever hoping you wouldn't do the same.
Constantly looking over her shoulders, trying to convince herself that you will actually remain.
A lesser woman would not mind lifting you up to keep you pleased.
She would just have to live with the fact that you could always do her the same way that you did me.
Or maybe that's exactly what you need.
A lesser woman that will make you feel more like a man, not a woman that was not content with just letting you be.

Made in the USA
Columbia, SC
24 December 2018